Speaking

Without Interruption

I0099953

an Essay

By P. Brennon

ISBN 978 1-7355972-0-1

1st Edition Paperback

Distribution & Print Services

By

Kindle Direct Publishing

www.KDP.com

Manufactured and Printed in

The United States of America

Speaking Without Interruption

****

Prologue

You know when you're passionately laying out your two cents, and you realize that your audience is not really listening – but shaking their head uh-huh waiting to jump in with their own opinion? Before you finish a paragraph or tie it all together? Then you're so flustered that you really don't get to hear what they're saying either. Well, a little bird suggested I just write it all down.

What we visually see is interpreted through our mental filters and latent influences. After all, you can't see yourself from where you're standing.

Important people tell us what they think. Insiders tell us what they know. Scholars write intellectual text.

The little people, the nobodies, the middle class -the silent majority- have opinions too.

****

Speaking

Without

Interruption

Table of Contents

INTRO

Penning my thoughts allow me to state my opinion without being interrupted.

It's just common sense opinions, nothing that you didn't already know. Hearing it again could bring it back to your attention, with the repetition activating ideas previously overlooked in all the minutia and neon that bombard us every day.

PSYCHOLOGY

I worry about the desensitization of America through the accelerated erosion of decency, ethics, and lawfulness. The hypocrisy of religion.

Of all the sciences, I find psychology to be the most interesting.

Desensitization, meaning to make one insensitive or non-reactive to stimuli through constant exposure to it, normalizes behaviors that were previously intolerable. We no longer *expect* ethical practices. The 'spin' has been normalized.

Desensitization can also be positive – constant exposure to interracial couples, gay people, disabled persons, and multiple races don't even turn our heads. It's normal now.

Assimilation refers to the process of acquiring the habits and lifestyle of the host or dominant culture, or one group mixing into another. Many Americans want no mixing and fraternizing, while others demand other cultures conform (assimilate) to their ways, period. The rest of us let people be themselves as long as they don't interfere with our own life choices.

Still another term – *internalization*, is to incorporate a value or fact or situation into one's self- consciousness as guiding principles acquired by learning or socialization. One can learn facts and see things – but they haven't internalized them (let it guide their behavior) until they realize and accept that it effects them personally. It's like with the Covid-19 virus – a lot of people behave badly because they internally believe that it's a thing that affects *other* people or since they never experienced real viral danger, they rationalize that it's no different than a bad cold. Something they could handle. It takes a lot of rationalization.

Psychology even plays a role in racism.

There are many reasons why we still have bigotry today, the *least* of which is disdain for an entire race. Most often it's about economics - feeling that a new group is sucking up all the jobs, feeling that funds being spent on other groups should be used for other things, being denied access to something that would be of great benefit to you, restricting access to something because you don't want to share the benefits. Sometimes it's about personal jealousy and envy. Feeling you should be living better than *those* people, or that others are taking the spotlight. Similarly, it could be the result of a *superiority* complex, where you are okay as long as the other group doesn't think they are as good as you are. Then there's the really low self-esteemed people who need to make others appear small just to make themselves appear adequate or bigger.

There are also those emotionally disturbed people who just want to fight. They will join any cause that gives them a cover to hurt people or to grandstand. There's the mimicking of behavior learned from family members who in word, deed, or subtle action imprint the bias onto other family members. There is peer pressure to fit in well with the people closest to you or to keep your job. Racism is often exacerbated for political and/or financial reasons.

Real racial hate may come from the difference between telling a child that his father died in war serving his country or saying that (for example) Germans killed his father. It also could stem from being secluded long term from people who are different, then having your first encounter go severely wrong.

So – which reason fits your biases?

What *motivates* you and what is most important to you – is information that can be used to control you. When your emotional needs are known, you can be manipulated. You need only to look at the advertising/marketing environment and at what's been happening in our current political environment to understand the relevance.

Psychology is deep.

RELIGION

It seems like one of the greatest failures of the church is not teaching people to be *grateful*. We tend to judge ourselves by the situation of others and lash out when we can't accept our own predicament. We don't value *ourselves*. In extreme cases, you think that you deserve what someone else has and since you can't have it – you try to make it where they can't have it either.

That's just wrong.

And if we were more grateful we'd be less *judgmental*. It's hard for the church to teach us *that* while religion itself is so judgmental.

Christianity has splintered off into so many sects that it's not really a single concept. Religion itself has become very politicized and competitive and capitalistic. A good percentage of religious leaders are womanizers, ambitious media hogs, supportive of whatever's popular, and after material success and/or celebrity. Some are serious activists while others just like all the press. And don't get me started on the character of some of the congregation.

It shouldn't be as shocking as it is that there is so much sexual misconduct in the Catholic Church. It's unnatural for a human being to be denied the 'nature' God gave us. This idea of marrying

God and being celibate for the rest of one's life is unnatural. Being allowed to have a mate and have children and be a part of a family is central to the well-being of any human. One would think it would make that person a better counselor.

Imagine years ago the church life and vows of celibacy being the perfect haven for those confused souls not knowing the reason why they were not interested in conventional relationships. Or those who could not accept what they saw as abnormal cravings turning to the church so they would not be able to act upon them and/or worrying that one might lose the love of their family or worst yet – be stashed away in some psychiatric facility to be 'fixed'. And then there's those who genuinely want to serve, those with so much compassion and empathy who know it's their calling. How would it manifest as the years go by never having the intimacy innately meant for everyone? Is it any wonder that Catholic school nuns were so abusive to their charges? Or the many cases of pedophilia? How strong our propensities must be that they would force one to abuse children.

Thankfully the current populace is much more educated on and accepting of sexuality and alternative lifestyles. We are better equipped to guide our children. *All* people are better equipped to live happy productive lives – a better alternative than depression, suicide, living secret lives, or just not having a life. A better alternative than being destructively judgmental or using your time spewing hate and insisting everybody be just like you. A better alternative to having people join the church for the wrong reason or having the church be the haven for abnormity.

We should just allow priests and nuns to marry (to whoever they want) as they perform their duties.

And it's time that we realize that pedophiles cannot be 'cured' or rehabilitated no more than heterosexuals or homosexuals can. It's their nature and we have to lock them away. It would be more humane to put them to sleep because they will never be allowed to have the relationship they crave legally, the intimacy humans deserve. It sounds harsh and I know we won't kill them. I just can't stomach any abuse of children.

I see so much hypocrisy in religion. I see a *lot* of it in *some* churches. I know so many 'church people' who are so offensive in their lives. I guess they go to church to show off their clothes and cars, some go to drum up business, others like to dress up and take their families out, with it being so much cheaper than some of the other places they could spend quality time with them. Some are just expected to go and it would be too much criticism if they didn't. So many phonies.

On the flip side, though, many people still go to church because they feel nearer to God there. They reflect on the sermon, enjoy the choir. It's a peaceful time for them. It's the only time they're not working and can just chill. Others find that sense of belonging when they find the right church. They participate in all the activities, become casual friends of the parishioners, sometimes volunteer at functions. It's their social life and it keeps them active and feeling safe. It makes them happy. Some are ambition or their activities make them feel needed or important – and what's wrong with that, especially if you don't feel it anywhere else. So yes, churches still have their place.

So much for parishioners. What really makes a church, of course, is the priest. Some are quite predatory with their need to be idolized and their constant push for more and bigger donations. I feel a church and its pastor must do more than just make sure you learn each verse of the bible. They should provide useful sermons that promote gratefulness, morals and ethics. They should remember that they somewhat speak for God, so no matter what their personal shortcomings are, must speak of righteousness from the pulpit.

If there's one thing you can say about the bible, it is always relevant through extrapolation to everything current. Some stories in the Bible remind me of

Aesop's fables. In his story about the Tortoise and the Hare, the moral is 'slow and steady wins the race' and it's not how fast you do things but how well, and that it doesn't pay to rush. When you hear in the Bible that the waters of the Red Sea parted so Moses and his people could walk across, escaping those chasing them, the moral of that story – the thing you should walk away with – is God can do anything and takes care of his people.

When Jesus says "let he who is without sin cast the first stone" the take away is to not be so quick to judge others (least ye be judged….) and that you are not perfect or better than anyone else, and that it's wrong to look down on others. Sure the Bible is an excellent tool for guidance when interpreted as such, but the goal of a good sermon is to enrich life, to help one live a better life spiritually and morally in deference towards all of God's people and creations. The world he built for us.

Don't equate money given to the church as money given to God. The money is given to a church/to the human leader. *Good works* being done with the donations by a church is the praise to God.

Religion has been the catalyst for many conflicts, wars, and manipulation. We study history but it seems we don't actually learn from it. There used to be so many idols and so many different Gods. Finally we settled on one God, but of many, many religions. Religion in its current form does not foster unity.

Speaking of psychology, religion, and gratefulness – it would be nourishing to forgive. Forgive *yourself.* We don't really tell people about those things from our past that we're ashamed of. But whether you know it or not, that shame affects you. Most often there's actually nothing to be ashamed of. It was done because you *honestly* thought it was the right thing at the time. Even if you immediately thought it wrong, a decision had to be made and you made it. You said something to someone that you wish you could've taken back or said differently. So now you know better.

But at the time… you didn't.

You can't expect that person from then to do or say what you *now* think after new experiences and passage of time. Something awful happened to you but you couldn't tell because you're so embarrassed or helped to cause it. But with what you know now, let yourself admit that it really *wasn't* your fault and things like that happen to almost everybody.

So let it go.

It helps to tell someone. It could be a complete stranger, someone you'll never see again that doesn't know anybody you know. The most important thing is you saying it out loud and looking at it again objectively. You could go into a Catholic church and confess it to a priest. If there's a confidant you trust that way –tell them about it. Say the whole thing *out loud*, and then let yourself resolve it. People pay psychologists good money to listen to them talk to themselves.

Fodder

Do you remember when water had no odor and was not so full of bubbles that you couldn't be sure you rinsed off the dishes? I wonder if the boards and managers of the water plants actually drink the water. I remember our first TV. It showed black & white and had 4 channels. Eventually, advertisement seconds were sold. The commercials were 30 seconds long and appeared in the middle of the show. Now there are hundreds of channels, and you have to pay extra to see the majority of them and you are pummeled with commercials throughout a single program, functioned to turn your volume up so you will hear if you step away.

Remember when you could stop by your cable provider, your phone

provider, the loan companies, and your apartment complex business offices to pay your bill? Well, now you have to pay large fees to do that. They prefer you pay without bothering them.
That's right, you have to pay them for bringing them their money.

Here's another notice from a software provider telling you they've 'updated' their policies and that continued use says you agree to these terms.
So.
I paid for the program. Now I'm coerced into allowing anything they want or scrapping my investment. It's demeaning, you feel insignificant and helpless, and learn to let more & more go.
So *many* people, adult and children, don't have access to computers or know how to operate them, and it's not just seniors. They're being locked out.

Products no longer come with instructions, some only supply them and other necessary information online. Courts and other disciplines tell you to get what you want or need online.

Instead of answering questions, they reply 'that information can be found on our website. There are free computer classes at senior and community centers, libraries and other places. An assistance area should be added for those who are just unable to 'get it', even if for a small fee. You'd think businesses would have alternatives available for those who need it.

Our value has been reduced to a marketing targets, period. Sales people are so friendly and helpful and nice – until after you buy something.

For as long as I can remember, when the question asks for the professions the least trustworthy, the answer is always Politicians, Lawyers, and Used Car Salesmen. We know it but we've become desensitized to it, so nothing is done about it. I know there *are* some good ones. They are hard to find and aren't the majority. I've been bit hard by all three.

The prime interest rate for businesses was recently lowered to almost -0-, but has any of them, mortgages, car loans, retailers – lowered the rates *we* have to pay? Any?

I watched in public hearings while attorneys told people not to answer subpoenas, or tell what they know. I watched them lie outright in court on behalf of their clients. I've watched them obstruct justice and commit serious conflicts of interest. Does the ABA (Bar Association) take their licenses or even reprimand them? Depends on who they are and/or who their clients are. I guess its primary function is to collect fees. No wonder there's so little respect for anything anymore.

Politicians lie alright. Little white lies, sometimes big serious lies. So we vote for the lessor of evils and allow the evil-doers to falsely malign those with some integrity. Car dealers charm you like snakes and after you leave you find you've been had. But the credo is 'buyer beware' as if the layman is supposed to keep up with all the laws of the day and not be such easy marks.

Point? It used to be that businesses tried to market things that would please the consumer and provide customer services to enhance the decision to purchase. The customer was always right, so to speak. Now, everything is manufactured to increase business income. They charge you extra for needed add-ons whose costs were not mentioned in the advertised price, and customer service is almost nonexistent. They don't want to answer their phones, they don't want to provide competent customer services, and charge huge late fees but don't feel like accepting your payment in person, or adjusting your bill when your service is out for a week.

Consumer protections barely exist and are rarely enforced. We become desensitized to it. We just go along, not knowing what else to do.

Didn't there used to be a consumer protection agency? What do they do? I know there have been several consumer protection laws passed. As soon as we turn our head, they're taken back. There was a law against usurious interest fees. Axed. Instead they instituted laws to make it harder to enter class action suits against huge businesses. If you do business in a state, consumers should be able to sue in that state, regardless of where you build your headquarters. If they don't have large business assets or enough liability insurance, they shouldn't be allowed to have limited liability (LLC's). Where's the incentive to run a quality business if you're not held personally responsible? Expiration dates should be on cosmetics since they *do* go bad. Holding Companies should have public records and transparency.

Generic medicines ought to be tested for content and reliability and not claim to be the same as a brand medicine unless it really is.

Remember when you were happy to get a job and that paycheck? Well, for a lot of people, getting paid for doing your job is not enough anymore. They want big bonuses either for just showing up or for cutting the job down to unproductive bones so as to have bonus money left. I just don't think it right for *government* employees to get bonuses.

You pay a great deal of money for your laptop, phone, tablet, etc. But you don't seem to own them. When companies feel like it, they change the programs. Just when you get everything set up to suit your purposes, they alter it. You don't have any control over it. There are updates, supposedly for security purposes, but during these updates other things also happen. Sometimes updates are run just to gather data on you. Or to install new sponsored apps, or place limits on things you can uninstall. It often benefits the providers more than it does consumer protection. Something always changes. I have no way of knowing when updates are truly for security.

Do you remember when cell phones came with 1 or 2 free games?

I recall the uproar over the federal government having access to your private correspondence, social media, telephone, and associations. If you aren't doing anything wrong, what's the problem? With everything on their plate, I don't think they'd find our day to day activities interesting at all. And if this helps them stop terrorism, sex trafficking, spies, corruption, child abuse, kidnapping – any of the things that *does* interest them, I support it. And I'll tell you, more people than you can count know more about you than you imagine, and all that knowledge is *sold* to other enterprises, legal or not. Check the internet about yourself. Pay a couple of fees to see what anybody who will pay will know about you, your family, your medical records, and your history. See how when you search for an item how many companies get your e-mail and/or FB page and/or your mailing address to show you their like products. And almost everything you want to use has lengthy technical usage and privacy policies that we all check off so we can get on with what we're doing. So basically, we've unwittingly approved it. That's why FB, Yahoo, G-mail and most everything else that's free *is* free. They widen their ad territory and collect data to peddle. It's a big profitable business. Other free offers are much more ominous, adding viruses or opening access to things on your system, etc., so beware. Once (that I noticed) after buying items from a large store and paying with my credit card, I immediately started getting coupons *in the mail* from them. My address was taken from my credit card records. Some might find this helpful, but just pointing out how many businesses and *their employees* have access to your information and know more about you than you realize.

I tip everywhere. I understand, you should help those poor people and reward their good service. Of course now it's just a thing. It doesn't matter if the service was not exceptional or even satisfactory. It doesn't matter how personable your waiter is. If you eat (or get your hair or nails done, etc.) it's now almost *mandatory* that you leave a tip. If there are multiple people at your table, the tip is computed *for you* and added to the bill. Now they even have tip jars at the take out cashier. And if your tip is not appropriate, you will be ostracized, get poor service and perhaps spit in your food.

Hotel and restaurant workers are not included in minimum wage laws. I guess because they get tips. *WE* are responsible for making their wage livable. The business owner's get rich but they don't have to pay their workers market or livable wages. What's wrong with this picture?

I give McDonald's credit for stepping up and raising the wages of their worker's, but just a little credit. After all, they didn't really take a big hit. They raised the prices of their menu items to cover the cost. Again, the burden falls on us. They can't raise prices much more, because the demand for their products will stop when the price gets too high. Don't get me wrong – there are a lot of employers who take good care of their employees. And it's out of profits. I still like McDonald's. I get really good service, decent fast-food, and I don't have to leave a tip. The extra I pay now is well worth seeing those nice servers get a decent wage.

Huge corporations often get away with murder. For example, take the companies that sell those 'flushable' wipes. The public service video on how items like these plug up the sewer systems have been shown on PBS, local government channels and other venues. The wipes can be flushed, but they are not biodegradable. Yet, they are still on the market. And it wouldn't hurt if restaurants and other users of bulk grease would have a separate container as hazardous waste to hold their used oils and have it dumped somewhere that doesn't go through the sewers to bind with other items that don't belong in the toilet.

Pharmaceutical companies and the government agencies that oversee them constantly leave us out of the loop and have unsavory practices.

Once medicine I needed was taken off the market and available months later in a different form. I paid for the product and in fact consumed it in my body. Yet I was not privy to any information from any source about the episode. And that's how it is with almost everything now. Pay and go away. No person or entity should be above the law. But that's not how it is.

We say we hate the disparities in income and that we need to help the underprivileged. Yet vital information television channels are not available without additional charges to all who would benefit from them. So the divide in education and social interaction is maintained. Those channels *should* be profitable but selling advertisement isn't enough? School systems in crowded, underfunded, disenfranchised areas are stuck with inferior education. Often, their parents are uneducated or focused on just getting by or self-medicating, or re-enacting harsh habits toward their children that they learned from *their* parents. In these dense areas, teachers and counselors and human resource systems are also understaffed, so there's just so much they can do.

Mandatory insurances and ever increasing license and traffic ticket fees keep many from having dependable transportation. It limits the things they can do, lessens their self-esteem and makes them appear as second class citizens. And why must the government hold themselves in higher priority and without restraint on amounts owed to them over other liabilities like retail rent, and utilities?

Most retailers and lenders add a late fee at the end of 30 days, yet traffic tickets add huge fees every two weeks. If a person had to save a little and take a day off work to attend to them – they'd find when they got there the tab had risen to 2 or 3 months' pay in just the matter of a couple of months.

The majority of politicians (not all, mind you) regardless of party, look right through you if they don't see an opportunity to collect money or obtain free labor for projects they will subsequently take credit for. Most people are not included in functions or information gatherings and can't afford the tickets for them anyway.
And so on. The poor are systemically kept poor. The middle class is being systematically lowered in stature.

There are even subclasses in the class divisions of poor, middle and upper class. I really hate it when people driving, watching cable TV, eating well, and *living* somewhere refer to themselves as 'poor'. Sure, they're low income, but they probably never interacted with the actual impoverished. Often, the well-to do consider themselves the upper class.

There are several classes of rich people. The rich, the ultra-rich, and the dynasty rich. As I don't interact much with any of the rich, I shouldn't elaborate.

Still, I have definitely noticed a difference in the suddenly newly rich and the dynasty (born) rich. Further, there is a huge difference between those who worked tirelessly starting from nothing to build their fortune, and those that were given everything in gala fashion from birth and have only associated with those of like lineage. The born rich weren't *born* evil –they just have no reference point to understand *other people*, no patience with them, an inbred disdain and little use for them. In a way, they're handicapped. There's no *real* work ethic even when they attempt entrepreneurial endeavors, over-funded by their abundance of…funds. There's little development of a moral center or the ability to see pass their own wishes. They've had everything the average person could ever have wanted so there's little to work towards or look forward to. So self-actualization will morph into goals alien to the average person. It's just no telling. If they become chronically insatiable, they'll excuse anything.

The government is the biggest contributor to inflation. (Not the only factor, but the biggest.) When laws are enacted for businesses – for the good of

the people or the country or the planet-
those businesses seldom lose money to
adhere to those regulations, they just
charge the consumer more. We pay for
it. I mean what respectable company
could tolerate clearing only 20 million
when they had always cleared 25
million? How embarrassing and scary
would it be to send their stockholders
two less dollars each in one year? So
things keep going up for us. Of course
when these businesses get a big hay
day, they never think to pass a tiny
portion of it back to their customers.

To give huge businesses a hand, when
government regulations require a big
costly equipment/procedural change to
fall into compliance – perhaps the
federal government could pay a third of
validated cost OR let the cost be
allocated as a subtraction from net
income before taxes are applied. The
government assistance would be

dependent upon the work being performed by arms-length American contractors through the bidding process, a work plan depicting completion, and no increase in consumer price. That way the entire expense won't be on the business and compliance would not contribute to inflation.

The government is sometimes like the old mafia. They see something making money and they want 'a piece of it'. They want in. The 'number men' were making so much money that the government moved in and 'took it over'. Now we play our numbers with the state alongside various other lotteries. Prostitution used to be illegal. But profitable. So the government stepped in, legalized, regulated and taxed it. The marijuana dealers were prospering, so that too was legalized, regulated, and taxed. I smell another tea party in the air….

Sorry – that's a bad parable while we actually have a crime family in control.

So the general population breaks down to fodder for use by retailers, corporations, advertisers, politicians, government and everybody else. The weight is on us. Pawns in various schemes. Shown little conscious or remorse, and having little recourse.

By letting so much go, letting so much 'slide', and increasingly lax adherence to laws – little by little the taking advantage of us has made the assaults more brazen.

Kudos

You know, I really have to give **Putin** credit for his ingenious plan to manipulate and disrupt the United States from the inside and to install his own lapdog as president. He probably would never have dreamed it would go so well so quickly! Consider all the facets – the methodical injection of propaganda and false facts to turn Americans against each other, to leave them accepting outrageous behavior in high office, to abandon people and ideals they'd once held dear. An evil genius.

And I have to give **Trump** a hesitant hand for using his polished grifting skills to pull off getting into the White House without getting votes, and using that position to increase his business interests and personal finance. Right in plain sight! How ingenious to secure the senate to shield and protect him in return for facilitating the republicans and lobbyists evil plan to 'fix' the courts with flunky judges that would protect he and McConnell, hold them above the law, and approve anything the lobbyists paid them for. And for being able to be even *more* criminal after impeachment!

And for his Nobel Prize: He managed to bring us the 1918 pandemic, the 1929 depression, and the 1968 riots all in one year! (And mismanaged them all.)

And kudos to Moscow Mitch 'the frog' **McConnell** for having the tenacity and gall to obstruct the duties of the Senate and the business of the people for years to this very day. And like Putin, I bet he never dreamed he could get away with so much for so long or that it would go so well so fast! To incorporate the Russian offensive into his plan and to skillfully force senate republicans to fall in line and abandon their pride, reputation, patriotism, and their constituents - unbelievable. He has obstructed every plan, bill, and funding that has anything to do with fighting foreign influence in our elections. Every one.

A shout out to the **NRA** who successfully washed all the contributions to Trumps campaign from Russia and acted as communications go-between. And for participating in a successful propaganda/advertising campaign themselves to attach the guns they sell to 1st amendment rights, and to further hypnotize nuts into thinking Democrats want to take their guns. It worked so well, they instigated it into the use of masks – as abusing one's freedom and constitutional rights.

I don't think you have the right to endanger other people's lives, whether to spread deadly germs, or put weapons into unqualified hands or automatic war weapons in general population. So it's okay for gangs to have automatic war weapons and be better armed than the police just so you can garner more sales contracts?

I never dreamed there were so many Americans with pent up anxieties and insecurities that would reveal so much racial bias and hate to the point of supporting repulsive activity for the gratification of seeing other people humiliated and hurt.

The people who came forward with information, those who were fired for telling the truth or disagreeing with horrible ideas, or just for making a criticism - are our country's HERO's. When this immoral reign is over, I hope we can reward and restore them.

And when the mental fog dissipates, we WILL remember this president and all the spineless enablers in congress, the agency officials, the wealthy 'donors', the NRA, and the white nationalists -all who tried to destroy our system of democracy in support of dictatorship, lowered our country's security, removed us from the world stage, put billions in the personal coffer of a crime family, discarded rules of law, discarded ethical precedents, abandoned foreign allies, sacrificed the lives of innocent immigrants and the lives of US/ Allies/veteran servicemen, abused immigrant children and came then after *our* children while under unsafe viral conditions, and left us alone and uninformed to fight a deadly pandemic - merely to appease a delusional criminal that would grant whatever anybody paid for, and for narcissistic political supremacy. They should be boycotted and shunned and punished. Hopefully prosecuted.

It's ironic how Trump instigated such racial bias, but that because of it in the 2018 elections the silent majority had to speak up by voting in Muslims and Blacks and Trans genders and Gays and any others that have been discriminated against and targeted by this administration.

Of course he didn't take the hint.

Pride

I find it ironic that this country was created by founders that took issue with their country charging excessive & abusive taxes without representation. Ironic that they decided not to work through the system to improve the situation, but ran off and created a country they could be boss of. That upon finding the perfect spot, took what knowledge from the natives they could use, and then brutally shooed them away. And lest we forget – settlements from Spain and France sided with the colonies and helped fight off the British, thus sealing our independence.

The first elections between two parties was in 1796. There were various parties that came and went, the Democratic Party being the oldest (1792) originally known as the Democratic-Republicans. Around 1860, this party split over differences – one being named the Democrats, the other being the Republicans. The two-party system of Democrat & Republican was formally cemented around 1924. It's interesting that during those times, it was the Democrats who were popular in the south and offended by talk of giving 'coloreds' any rights. The Republicans were popular in the North seeking to end slavery and give rights to the freed slaves. For years only white men that owned property could vote, then all white men could. In 1870 per the 15th Amendment, black men were allowed to vote (at least it was *legal*). The Ku Klux Clan originated in the south about then to keep blacks from voting. Then in 1920 the 19th Amendment gave women the right to vote (although a few states had already been allowing it).

In 1787, the three branches of government and the Judiciary Federal Courts were initiated.

The argument over powers of the federal government vs powers of the states has been going on since the late 1700's.

Republicans in the distant past gave us some remarkable presidents who made indelible positive marks on this country. Lincoln freed the slaves. Eisenhower created the interstate highway system, strengthened the programs in the New Deal, and provided additional protections for African Americans. He warned against the dangers in 'partnership' of the military and big business and partnership of government with big business. Roosevelt (Teddy) enacted the Federal income tax, ordered the *election* of senators, and busted down monopolies. It's just heartbreaking what republicans have become in the last 15-20 years. These guys would be so embarrassed. But…those guys had integrity and grit – they would have stopped it.

Franklin Roosevelt was a democrat. He created many desperately needed programs and agencies responding to the relief needed after the Great Depression. One was the Social Security Program. These were social reforms to take care of the citizens and raise the dead economy. Nobody called him a Socialist then. He served 4 terms. (Is that when Republicans limited presidents to just two terms?)

I'm an Independent. Sometimes I vote republican, sometimes democrat, occasionally independent. I don't recall voting for any of the other fleeting parties. I'm proud of trying to support the right *person* instead of a straight party. Recent events have made me consider closer what these 'parties' represent. It appears the republicans have morphed into a cult acting as one person. One corrupt traitorous power hungry greedy person. It's shocking, really. The democrats are trying to band together to support a presidential candidate, but other than that, appear to be a diverse group of many different minds, mostly tending towards helping the citizenry. The independents, green, feminists, and tea parties are being quiet. They appear to be taken aback by events of late, and siding with democrats to help set things right again.

I caught on to the great propaganda initiative that went into its planning stage the minute Obama won his second term. Stage one appeared to rouse tension against blacks and immigrants and exaggerate negatively acts of the then current president, and to circulate phony data and lies. The next step appeared to equate Hillary Clinton to the black evil president. What had been known for eight years as the 'Obama Administration' or the Obama/Biden Administration' was now referred to as the 'Obama /Clinton' administration. Even the press unwittingly picked up the term. It was figured out that Hillary would get the democratic endorsement long before it was final. They said the same things so many times in so many places that it felt true because you heard it everywhere. Then they trotted out this 'character' candidate who seemed exciting to watch and had good slogans. They stressed that America needed a businessman at the helm. He made fun of people, talked street, made irrational promises from the podiums. The lay folks had no way of knowing of his disastrous business skills, that he *couldn't* speak like an adult and knew few words, that he was a compulsive liar, that he had no credit and tons of lawsuits against him. They would never guess his ties with Russia. He was just fun, different, refreshing.

The people that are supposed to take care of the citizens and the country – they knew. They didn't like or trust him, but they would have a republican president. They set the vetting aside and ran with it. Even with all they knew about him. Even with the briefing from security people that he was expected of being a Russian asset. All they could think of was having a republican for president.

So the immoral, greedy, power-hungry heads looked the other way.

They thought they could steer him and that he'd learn fast. There was something they *didn't* know, that he was not interested in learning anything. That he would start pimping the presidency even before his inauguration. And continue it his whole term. That he'd place people in charge of important agencies that were just as incompetent as he, but would do whatever he wanted. Only Moscow Mitch McConnell knew these things. They were in it together. They continued to man the courts with their own guys so that McConnell could get rid of the ACA and reverse Roe vs Wade. Also to aid the new president in being above any laws. They gained the allegiance of other republicans to rush un-vetted candidates through so they would have the platform to advance the republican agenda. I think most of them still believe that was the motive.

McConnell was painfully aware that the citizenry did not want the ACA reversed. He had tried to strike it down in over 30 court hearings. He had failed, only getting a couple of small things removed, none that benefited the insured. Then, he ended up having control of *both* houses in congress and still couldn't get a reversal approved by them. So it's safe to say that *nobody* besides the lobbyists that were paying and funding him to get rid of it wanted it. And they were fuming by now.

But who cares what anybody else wanted? Now McConnell could take it to court on his own without congress and have his judges finish it off. His handlers had paid mounds of money for a very long time to get rid of the ACA. The Roe vs Wade was also a stern request from huge evangelical donors.

He didn't care what Trump wanted out of it, besides sanctioning his own overt criminal activity. And that of his criminal associates. McConnell could care less about that.

Look where we are today. Look what we *all* know about Trump, McConnell, the NRA, and the Republican Party as a whole. In the news is his failure to handle the pandemic and the additional deaths he caused through lies, inaction, and obstruction. So much so that we tend to forget the other monstrosities that he perpetrated. So, so many that it makes your head spin, desensitizes us to the reality of it all.

We've had to face some facts about people we thought we knew, about people in general, about things that have been manifesting all along that we were too involved in our own little world to see. It's disheartening, to say the least. Most of us probably left the running of the country and commerce, to those who knew how to handle it – knowing that once something hit the fan on the upper middle class, changes would be made that would eventually flow down to the rest of us in the spirit of keeping up the appearance that we are all equal. Then suddenly you have to pull your head out of the sand and are shocked at what you see!

What the….

It's hard listening to people who aren't offended by the behavior of this administration and the fabricated spins they put on, and how they've turned this country into a criminal dictatorship. It hurts seeing well-meaning people fall for it. It sucks that some people will allow *anything* as long as they see people they want to be better than get shafted. Or anything as long as they keep receiving those stock dividends. It's upsetting to have to wait to vote them out, because EVERY DAY Trump is in office it's a different stunt to lose the support and confidence of allies and create new enemies, to harass innocent people, to promote ciaos & bigotry and civil unrest, to promote Russia's agenda, to run the country into debt we may not be able to get out of, to disrespect the office of the president and denigrate federal agencies, to sabotage national security, to harm children (immigrants AND ours), to ruin the reputation and respect of those who stand around him, *to publicly dupe citizens with deliberate harmful lies*, to get rid of all moral government workers, and remove restrictions and responsibilities for donors and businesses. EVERY FREAKING DAY.

It's easy for knowledgeable people to manipulate others. A whole national network (Fox News) joined in the effort, bots that seemed like regular people at first, permeated social media, another cable network ran by Russia (OAN) stepped in to make Fox News not be the only one saying this stuff. And we all have our own emotional and egotistical needs that can be heightened through this manipulation. Still, everyone is entitled to their opinions, manipulated or not.

But if at this late date after all we *actually* know, you support trump and his flunky senate and appointees, you support public habitual lying, theft, bribery, coercion, extortion, corruption, bigotry, promotion of civil war based on hate and sadism, abuse of children, abuse of adults, murder of journalists, murder of allied forces, murder in commission of hate crimes, murder of our soldiers, dictatorship, absence of any laws, Russian interference in our government, suppressing voting, tampering with ballots, taking away healthcare from millions of citizens, taking away social security from seniors, pay-to-play by 'donors', constant manipulation of the economy that can't be sustained and will devastate it, agencies and institutions run by unknowledgeable greedy corrupt flunkies, alienating this country to the world stage, losing our allies for the favor of American enemies, using our armies to clear the way for Russian aggression in other countries, and so much more. Notwithstanding the blatant disregard for American lives during this pandemic. If you support that I could never respect or trust you. Not ever.

I could never forgive the republican congress for allowing all this. I pray not one of them ever be elected again, and that they go to jail for complicity in the dangerous criminal and treasonous acts of this administration.

I realize that at first some of you thought you were doing the right thing. Some of you felt good about those vague but psychologically enhanced biases (until it was taken too, too far). Some of you probably believed the hype, thinking the fault lay in others and that everybody had it in for the president because he was a republican and/or because they just didn't like his policies. Some of us found the constant news of new wrongdoing surreal. Fabricated. After all, it was done in plain sight. **But *it's not believable that you don't know better by now*.**

Sadly, some of us thrive on ciaos, bigotry, instigating trouble and sadistic fighting. Some are hard core racist or pretend to be to join the conflict. Some will support this stuff even by sacrificing the country and their own life. I feel so sorry for them. Except that they're taking me down with them.

And as Covid-19 unfolded, again I was faced with being stunned by people. Trump has made it cool to go against the laws, to discount anything a democrat says, to internalize the propaganda they've been fed about their 'rights'. Adults that think it is okay for laypeople to have weapons of war and there should be no regulations attached to gun ownership. Despite the proliferation of gangs and murders and mass shootings. Grown people who have such low self-esteem that they parade in armed groups in order to intimidate. People like that don't believe in anything – just inciting conflict. They want an excuse to hurt people. There's no telling what circumstances in their lives were so disappointing and demeaning to make them be like that. People who are unwilling to wear a mask to protect themselves and those around them, to facilitate the end of this scourge. They scream about their rights (really?) and how they want things opened up. Yet they won't do what's necessary to make it happen. They are hopelessly unaware that all this 'rights' stuff was put in their heads by the NRA with Russian support and co-signed by our current presidential administration. They don't seem to realize that they are sacrificing their very lives. And for what? They don't seem to realize that all they are to republicans is a vote; and that they can be discarded afterwards. We watch grown men kicking down doors after the government locks them down. As with the president – no respect for laws; no respect for democrats – the only people trying to help them. It blows my mind.

After this is over and people speak of their loved ones that died from the virus and television documentaries go back over all that has happened, they will cringe when they see how they behaved. They'll see how their friends and family and neighbors and strangers regard them.

How will they regard themselves?

I don't think anybody has a right to disobey the law. Especially when in doing so you harm others. We have to use common sense. Have some pride.

Criminal Justice

My attitude now is if the police say halt, and you take it upon yourself not to –that's on you. If you're caught roughing up and robbing an old person, I don't have time to worry about some officer smacking you with a stick even if it's not the correct action. If a cop has to chase you and when he catches you, you want to struggle and fight and hurt them to get away – they should do what they have to do to get you off the street *and* make it home whole. We have to remember that police officers are *people*. If you saw a thug knocking your mother to the ground and ripping her purse away, you'd chase him. What would you do when you caught him?

I bet you'd try to beat him to death until you caught yourself. Because it sickens you to see her being preyed upon. Well, police officers are sickened by it too. They have mothers and children and old folks. Luckily, they're trained and can hold in their emotions better than we can and aren't allowed to do what we would do. But they have to coddle these habitual ingrates every freaking day. I can definitely understand a little loss of cool. I'm tired of all the crime. Tired of mannish thugs that don't have respect for anything. Tired of being hesitant to walk outside with my money or dry cleaning. Tired of my car and/or garage being broken into. The flagrancy of it.

Still, since I'm not an animal I'm glad there are people out there investigating these cases just in case there really was unnecessary abuse, and weeding out the badged sadists. Yes, a lot of the bad cops are racist, but a lot are people who need to boss people around, who like to feel power, who like to inflict pain and punishment. And those types are abusing any disenfranchised person they run across regardless of race.

After that last 'choke hold' death, it was so heartwarming to see all races marching together against systematic racism against blacks and police brutality against them. And all over the country it was happening despite our corrupt president stoking racial bias. Governors and other statesmen came to realize what confederate flags and statues must feel like to black people – and had them removed. It was established that officers who witnessed and allowed police brutality would also be punished as abettors. All good.

We're watching. *All of us*.

Of course the attention getters chose to ride this wave for their own aggrandizement by taking it too far.

They added some violence to the peaceful marches, they organized looting, and they wanted more statues removed that were not confederate. They accused some ex-presidents of owning slaves, which was the norm for landowners in those days. They cried for defunding police departments, when everyone had been crying for months to hire *more* police officers to handle the myriad of crimes happening in cities. It is one thing to wish to have more social services funded, but another to take it from the police. The interlopers hollered for this and that and made me afraid that the groundbreaking strides blacks gained in this movement would be compromised. None of this additional complaining was what the majority of black people wanted at this time. With most police stations around the country trying to improve citizen relations and starting to weed out offenders, I wonder how these ideas made the officers who put their lives on the line every day feel.

We have to be careful not to tie law enforcements hands. When I was younger, a stop & frisk law was instigated in response to the high level of criminal activities and murders. The idea was to get criminals and gang members off the street. But it was too inconvenient for the 'good' people (who complained the loudest about something needing to be done) that resented being pulled over. They accused the police of targeting blacks. To be truthful, the cities and crime areas where these laws were activated were 80% black. Left unnoticed were the whites also arrested.

At some point, somebody got hurt or killed during a police high speed pursuit. Everyone forgot about the criminal that caused it and the uproar was over high speeds chases of the police. Law enforcement departments have rules in place that lay out when to chase and when to let it go. It's ridiculous to announce to criminals that if they drive fast, they can get clean away! We will get rid of the bad cops – *everybody* is on board with that. Don't blame the decent ones that are the majority. The police and the community *need each other* to strive.

I've almost always believed in the death penalty. Always appalled at the years these people stay in prison on our dime before meeting their fate. It may be more humane to let them die (by drugs, not electrocution or hanging) than to keep them locked up with no chance of release.

But…I've noted several real cases where the guilty person was *proven* to be innocent. I've seen successes by the 'Innocents Project' and other concerned citizens. I've seen several real instances where egotistical prosecutors refused to go back on their original reasoning, some even in the face of irrefutable evidence. So now I don't think they should receive their punishment so fast. One to five years should be enough – one if nobody can find a reason for appeal or new evidence *and* an arms-length confession was given. (Usually a mere confession can take the death penalty off the table-ugh). More time if there are appeals or new evidence proven accurate and each state's Appeals court designated 2 days a month for these life or death motions and hearings to help the process be more timely and humane. So much crime.

Unfortunately, there are people who shouldn't be allowed to walk freely among decent people. There's something wrong with a person who can viciously beat a human being for little or no reason. Or use *excessive* physical brutality while committing common crimes. Often, the question is 'did mental illness cause him do these things'? A lot of valuable court time is taken up investigating this. Being high on crack or being just put on a strong medication certainly are mitigating circumstances. But when a person kills an innocent stranger, or lock people up in a basement and kept them as pets or set fire to homes where families lie sleeping or are serial murders – of course they're crazy! But what if they *are*? They should still never be released into the population again. How many times have insane people been released and believed to be better and then did the same things several more times before being caught and given the life sentence or death penalty *then*? Your true nature cannot be stifled. We shouldn't take that chance.

Prison has to be humane but still serve as *punishment*. How many times has a person been charged with something heinous and has a long criminal history with jail time that escalated into his current charge? They were not turned away from crime after prison time and in fact were better equipped to do more without getting caught and weren't effectively afraid of prison – where they perhaps had friends and were assured of having meals and a steady warm bed.

Oh, my prison would be different. I have never appreciated how locked up, under guard criminals could have drugs, fights, rapes, and kingpins. What kind of prisons are these? There should be random drug tests by outside oversight and the guards for that area should all be fired if drug use is found.

No prisoner should be shown more respect and favor than them all. If attempted fights and sexual misconduct happens, the perpetrators should be confined to quarters for one or two weeks, and transferred to higher security facilities in a location not conducive to meeting former cohorts if being confined to quarters doesn't work.

My prison would not be privately owned and managed. The State would run it with federal oversite. Too many offenses in the prison, like drugs and fights, etc., would result in removal of the warden. Empathetic do-gooders would not have a prominent voice in making things exceptionally comfortable for inmates.

Without physical or mental cruelty, my prison would not be a vacation....

Breakfast, lunch and dinner would be served, but meat served only once a day. Coffee or juice would come with breakfast, water provided for lunch and dinner. There are great ways to make meals tasty and balanced nutritionally without serving meat or having sugar filled drinks. Each dinner would have a small dessert. An evening snack would be an actual piece of fruit. Classical music selections would play in the background until 'lights out'. Maybe do-gooders could provide holiday side dishes.

It'll be good for them.

Each cell would have a very comfortable cot on the floor, a window seat, toilet corner, and enough room to do moderate exercises, more with the cot stood against the wall. A small built-in shelf would hold letters and photographs, maybe a book from the prison library. Street clothes will not be worn, clean uniforms will be provided at each twice a week shower assignment.

Prison would be busy. We'd have two movie theaters. Through the weekdays, educational programs – National Geographic, The Learning Channel, The Discovery Channel, the Science Channel, Animal Planet, Body Bizarre, Mystery Diagnosis, Mysteries at the Museum, and the like. Interesting, thought provoking television. No Crime or other reality shows, no news, occasional cartoons. On the weekends there will be movies. Some comedy, some classics of all genres. You get four hours of educational TV a week and a movie once every two weeks.

There will be a library, just books. A book club to meet once a month to discuss the last book and receive the next. There will a class in reading, writing, and arithmetic. Entry orientation will insist on it for some, others may choose it.

You will be outside (in what is sometimes referred to as the yard) for walks, tennis, card games, checkers, and an aerobics session twice a week.

That's right. It's prison.

Besides Library/classes, showers, TV and movies, yard time, Lunch (the only communal meal), and visits – you remain in your cell, where breakfast and dinner will be served. A maintenance schedule will be set for 'room service' to disinfect surfaces and change bedding while a prisoner is out for their scheduled activities.

Visitors can see you only once a month by skype and twice a year for prescheduled in-person visits. You can have a whole family in your skype visits, only two with no children for in-person visits. A computer room in the prison, and a small room in the main Police Station in each city would facilitate skype visits. You can receive prescreened mail and write, but won't be able to receive money, clothes, food, or gifts while incarcerated. Now that would be prison.

Initially, and this is key, one would arrive and be placed in orientation for 30 to 45 days. Here you will adjust to the menu and adopt regular sleeping habits once you're safely weaned off drugs and/or cigarettes, neither of which will be allowed. They'll have more time to get used to being clean after they're transferred to lockup.

They'd have a medical review, a psychological examination, and an education evaluation.

You will learn not to be loud and *never* to use curse words. You will not be allowed out of your orientation cell until all of this has been accomplished. Then you'll be schooled on the routines in regular lock-up, and happy to be going there.

One thing that alienates released prisoners from regular people on the outside is the manner of language they acquire while incarcerated. The curse words seamlessly permeate every sentence, and they aren't aware that it's offensive.

The last two months should acclimate a prisoner to work life. There could be jobs in the kitchen, on the maintenance crew, and in the library. None of that 'furlough' stuff. Add evening yard time and extra TV and movie time on the weekends. With just a few weeks to be until release, there should be little incentive to make trouble or escape.

Parole officers would be advised of releases a month in advance so they can read and update the file on a prisoner and check the home situation to determine the steps that should be taken once released. A good parole office should already have a portfolio of willing employers, boarding and halfway homes, and associated to a Humanitarian Association (the goody two-shoes) that will assist a parolee in obtaining new eye glasses, dental work, clothing, etc. Parole would be six months.

The benefit of this system is tri-fold.

First, although inmates weren't harmed, they'd prefer being on the outside.

Second, the regular sleep and meal routines and not being dependent on drugs or cigarettes will have a healing effect on negativity and aggressiveness. Third, watching the educational series and seeing classic, *basically* non-violent movies will broaden the mind and insert new things to talk about as well as advance openness to learning new things. The quiet non-threatening environment and background music will make loud, threatening, negative environments less acceptable. After an excitable celebration at release, I believe a person would fall back to adhering to a regular healthy pattern that doesn't leave a lot of room for 'night crawling'. Also, prison would cost the government and taxpayers less money.

And if all this makes an impact when the criminal is incarcerated early- if they're not mentally ill-they might give up crime for a job and safe, more stimulating friends and activities! They would have marginal if any, contact with other offenders. Sentences would have to be 18 months to three years to be effective, shortening the total time for taxpayers to foot the bills, not promoting institutionalism, and hopefully cutting down on repeat offending.

Of course there should be a stricter facility for third time offenders, 'life' quarters, and death penalty cells – all three separate and never any mingling together in any fashion. These hard heads should have the same treatment, especially orientation, but should only be allowed out of their cells, except in the yard, a shower, and TV/movies twice a week each. The cart can bring books and they can exercise in their cells. Those sentences could be somewhat shorter, too. It will be so unpleasant, that, with the right exit strategy, could make them think twice about having to come back.

This model was made with men in mind, but needs just a little adjustment for women. As you've seen, a lot of them make formidable criminals and can be just as brutal.

Murderers are the worst offenders, although shooting a person with a gun is less brutal than beating a person to death or stabbing someone. A judge would be the one to assign the proper facility in cases where the death penalty didn't come in to play. Premeditated, grisly murders and those done while committing another crime are considerably worse than killing your spouse when you walk in unexpectedly and find them humping somebody else. That's *temporary* insanity... not much chance of them committing murder again. Life sentences should be eliminated. If a person needs to be locked up for life but didn't get a death penalty, he should have a right to request his life be ended peacefully by prison officials. It's inhumane to lock a human being away for life even when it's imperative to remove them from society. They become super institutionalized *at our expense* and have no ties on the outside if they are released before dying in prison. Besides, when you're in for life anyway, there's no incentive to be a model prisoner.

Sex offenders, now there's a filthy lot. They should have a bit more time in the higher security prison. And a bit more psychotherapy to determine if they should ever be released, but after the psychological lock up, there should still be some jail time on top to be safe. Realize some can't be rehabilitated.

Pedophiles – I under no circumstance think they can be cured. That's their nature. You can't accurately judge a person's behavior after release based on their behavior in captivity. I'm not talking about an 18 year old dating a sixteen year old. No. I'm talking about abusing children and grown men courting kids under 16. It's so *sick* to me, but apparently seems perfectly right to them. I feel sorry for them because they can't seem to stop and will have to live their lives unsatisfied or as a criminal. I think it would be kinder to put them to sleep, but I can already hear the objections. Maybe there should be a separate facility (maybe an island) to house them with some sort of factory attached where they could work and live old prison style with dining room meals, rec rooms and exercise rooms and adult family visits. Just no pay for their work, with the business they work for contributing to their room and board. No access to children. Doctor access for legal suicide if requested. Notice they are flight risks.

With all the efforts being made to make law enforcement unbiased and conscience of requirements to use brutal force, we ought to make some effort, too, to support them and law enforcement in general. This wide spread disrespect has to be tampered down. Snitching is an ugly word – intimidatingly made so by criminals who don't want to pay for their crimes. We can only hire and pay so many police officers. If I saw an ingrate knock an old lady to the ground and then take her purse and run – would you want me to tell the police who it was? Would I be a lousy snitch? If you knew who committed a crime or saw someone you knew the police was looking for would you let them know when there is no danger for you in doing so?

If not, you're part of the problem.

In area's with the least crime and the fastest officer response (because they don't have to wait for back-up.), people in that community work *with* the police in crime fighting. They take phone footage of the officers, too, but they don't put their phones aside while the perpetrators commit the crimes. They don't sneer and shout obscenities at the police when they swoop in to do their jobs. They back away from crime scenes and assist in any way that does not cause them or the officers any harm. *Nobody* expects or wants laypeople to be heroes. The very least good thing you could do to help is to get out of the way and let the police do their job without being nervous about watching their backs against crowd harassment. Help law enforcement help you if safely possible. Police often give their lives for our protection*, but dying is not in their job description and whatever they have to do to escape it is justified.*

By the way – a snitch to me is a person who tells who your spouse is hanging out with or tells when somebody was late - petty crap-starting stuff like that. A person who reports on safety hazards, suspected child abuse, spousal abuse, suspicious activity, a crime or a wanted criminal - is a **hero.**

I'm so glad these phone films have exposed the awful deaths by police of innocents or people who did not deserve to die. Many who weren't aware or couldn't believe it was happening, thinking criminals asked for it while fighting police – were shocked and offended by the behavior. Shocked at the innocent ones being killed. If it was a mistake, let it be the last by removing them or charging them with reckless homicide. If it was in flagrant disregard of procedure, send them *and* their enablers to prison for murder. ***Always*** withhold judgement until all the facts are in. I would rather have the police officers go home alive than waste that split second wondering about liability while interacting with dangerous people in this dangerous job.

If I were King....

As president-*elect* I would already have the names of my appointees. I would have already spoken to them about it. They would already know who their second in command would be as well as their chief assistant of whichever appointments required of such positions. I would already have spoken to my 'Cabinet' and chief 'advisors', had them screened for security clearance, and have their documentation and disclosures filed and at the ready. We will all make our tax returns available and be divested of meaningful business attachments.

Maybe this is how it's always been done. I would have made *sure* that everyone was well qualified and experienced at the task I've assigned them. The top of the country is no place to 'cut your teeth'. The department heads to be replaced will have their security clearance revoked. All simultaneously without warning. After all, they're criminals and traitors unlike previous appointees. No honor.

As president, the new appointees will meet with the Vice President and I with their prospective agency breakdowns – showing department's function and budget, pay rates, and any opinions they might have about it, where change may be needed, and who should stay or go – and why. The professionals I will have assigned will be able to formulate and install new people and plans in 6 to 10 weeks while still keeping operations going.

I would start WH attorneys into researching and formulating opinions on a few urgent cases. When Moscow

Mitch McConnell changed the rules of appointing judges as a means of making the process partisan and to allow rushing undocumented appointees through – was that legal? Could unlawful appointments be rescinded? If parts of the investigative security reports on a candidate were withheld from congress – are those appointments even valid? The answers to these questions will dictate how I would go ahead and have my choices appointed. No 'fast shoo-ins', though, but with thorough vetting.

How fast could the new boss of the post office be prosecuted and made to return or replace equipment stolen from the federal post office? How would we remove the current Board?

Our national and cyber security protocols will all have to be re-vamped.

We know of Putin's influence over this president regarding military matters, we know for a fact that he gave Turkish visitors top secret information in the oval office, and we know he shared technology with the Saudis shortly after that reporter was murdered by them. But so much we don't know. Scary.

So.... appoint a committee/task force to look into and write a bill to "Prevent corruption, Erosion of Ethics, and Despotism in the Federal Government" that would be submitted to both houses of congress to be approved. There would be language that a president, vice president, senator, or representative CAN be charged with a crime (indicted) and removed immediately (for everyone's safety) but be re-instated without harm if found not guilty (unless congress finds something found in the trial is a breach of ethics or security or some such and decides to impeach and remove). The criminal acts will be named, including fraud, bribery, extortion, obstruction, lying to congress and/or law enforcement, nondisclosure of material facts on required documentation, conspiring, aiding or abetting others who commit crimes. The trial would be in the courts. Also the act of doing things that should be approved by congress without obtaining that approval and breaking the emoluments clauses (which should be spelled out in plain all-inclusive, language) will be illegal. These things will be actual crimes and prosecuted. Consequences of each should be spelled out (fines, jail time, length of time to not be able to hold any office in government, etc.), with NO exceptions. When found guilty of a *crime*, there will be no need for a lengthy impeachment trail–it's automatic along with removal from office.

And speaking of impeachment… all non-criminal acts – which also must be spelled out such as lying to the American people on material facts, physically or mentally being unable to handle the office (of president, vice president, senator, or representative), making foreign deals that on their face are detrimental to the country and opposite of policy and not approved by congress, failure to answer questions of congress and congressional committees, and unethical behavior. These things would require a congressional hearing to show fact and/or mitigation as to whether or not they are true cause to impeach the person from office, by the finding of 2/3s of the vote (of both the house *and* senate). If impeached, removal would be mandatory.

Lobbyists will be forbidden from entering the WH. And they would be in Congressional offices by appointment only as noted at the front desk of the building. No more walking around like you own the country.

Another task force would look into the rules of activity in congress. We all know that senators are only required to meet 9 days, and only do more in cases of emergency.

They get paid well and have expense accounts and plush government offices at taxpayer expense. They have tricks to obstruct progress. These should be eliminated so congress can do its job of taking care of the nation's business.

There would be term limits on congressional offices, and on the speaker positions. If a bill is introduced by any congress person, it must be heard within thirty days and voted on in both houses to become actual law. The Senate or House will not be able to unilaterally make or remove laws or appoint anyone to a position. The congressmen should change to meeting for one week a month, having three weeks to examine and research the bills introduced. If it is voted necessary to extend a vote, it can only be tabled until the next month and then voted on for good. There will not be just a single person deciding whether or not a bill should be heard. They will all be heard. There will be no lesser bills piggybacking off the presented bill and each bill must have the name/names of the sponsors of the bill. Bills will not be sitting on anybody's desk gathering dust into eternity. Things will get done.

Congressmen have access to the best authorities on every imaginable subject and a tad of experience of their own. They have ample time to confer with their constituents both business and consumers. It shouldn't take months to decide a well written bill. Lobbyist should not be their only information. If they are taking illegal contributions or taking kickbacks or outright bribes – if they have offshore accounts that have not been disclosed- if their family members are getting new cars and unlimited credit cards, etc.,- they can be charged with a crime and removed from office.

It just angers me that a budget is due every year, yet, almost every year they act like it's a dire surprise emergency. They use it to make deals. They throw in bills that have nothing to do with the budget to get approved with the budget. Bills so crappy that nobody puts their name to them. The budget should be done and approved a good month before the deadline and posted so all can see it. We may not know what's good for the country budget wise, and if somebody does have input they should give it long before it's due. We deserve that as much as we deserve to see the tax returns of the people handling our money and our lives.

The senate Ethics, Intelligence, Appropriations, Foreign Relations, Judiciary, and Rules and Regulations committees, among others, are a joke. Oversite?? Joke.

They should all be merged into one committee with members from both houses that have legitimate security clearance, plus a person designated by the president, the OBM, and the AG's office. Of this 15-20 member committee, two or three each can be assigned (not the dept. appointees) major responsibilities for each concern such as foreign relations, ethic, judiciary, etc. They would give their respective reports at the meetings so all would be briefed and discussions can take place and actions worked out. There would be rotating Chairs, and no lobbyist or outsiders allowed at any meeting, except for info and testimony reasons at hearings. Agency and military officials can be called in to provide clarity and instruction in their areas. All other Congress people and government officials (with good security clearance) can read the minutes. This system would provide more transparency, bipartisanship, and less expense. *The powers of this committee would be legitimized and enforced by law.*

One of the things that stood out to me about our former President was that he acknowledged the working poor. An immediate payment was sent to them, and income requirements for food stamps were raised. Many who had complained about people getting them and seen them as moochers and scammers all, suddenly were applying themselves, even if they didn't tell anybody or admit to it. Naturally the price of groceries went up.

I would *immediately* appoint a Covid-19 committee consisting of CDC, Dr. Fauci, and WHO officials to advise me of what steps should be taken and what assistance was needed from me. I would have a W.H. liaison office staff with authority to make those things happen and give the Vice President and myself constant reports. A temporary committee from Treasury, HHS, OBM,

ACLU, & alternating guess governors will, with haste, create a stimulus and rescue plan and how to execute it to get help to the unemployed and all affected negatively by the virus situation. I would start FEMA and the Red Cross on collecting data about weather and fire devastations and formulate a solid plan for assistance to them, as well as assistance protocols for future catastrophes. All these operations will update and utilize the liaisons office.

I had always believed the Electoral College was a good thing and a safety valve in choosing a president. I never realized that these votes could be partisan or bought or thrown whatever way the electorate chose. Noting that they voted in a person with no experience, of questionable character, in trouble with law officials, being sued for fraud left and right, an illiterate lazy loud con man with a terrible business record – proves this system needs to be eliminated or re-vamped.

I believe the Supreme Court recently ruled that they had to cast their votes with the majority of the people's votes.

The Justice Department would be busy prosecuting newly available felons…..

In my first months (while the tasks forces and agency heads work their magic) I'd have a meeting with the party leaders of both houses to see and set the landscape. I would be open and honest with them. Then, I and my VP would meet with reputable foreign affairs people to catch up and strategize. Afterwards, we along with the appropriate ambassadors will speak to each president of our allies, and then to the other countries. Those first 3 or 4 months will hopefully set the tone of my term in office. Daily briefings would be read and thoroughly considered. One would think that goes without saying, but…..

And thus armed, down to the excruciating and rewarding business of running the country - with the WH cleared of corruption, treason, and disabling management ciaos. And together with both houses of congress, get things done.

Speaking of both offices of congress, they should be restored to their original status as equal bodies of power. We've seen what could happen when one body possesses more power. Or when a Chair works unilaterally. Or when one house or party high-jacks the entire government. Appointments to offices that have to be approved by congress must have an okay from *both* houses. Each chamber that sponsors a bill must be approved by both houses. Each house must consider and vote on these items in the required time period, and short summaries should be recorded as to why each individual voted yay or nay and be of public record. The power of each house to issue subpoenas or take similar actions must be sacrosanct, although these actions probably will be taken by the Main Committee. The VP will still have that tie-breaker vote when necessary.

I see a sketchy plan to fix social security. Raise the ceiling for the last time for income paying into the system still matched by employers. No personal income exempt, regardless of other retirement plans. (Politicians of all offices would contribute up to the income ceiling.) From the annual budget, an additional half billion should be transferred to the social security fund as reparation for the monies 'borrowed' from the fund by the government that was never paid back in, until the fund is deemed 125% funded. The declaration must be made not to touch that fund for non-social security purposes. And anybody with a proper payment record should be able to collect at age sixty-five if they choose to. At the existing payment rates plus C.O.L.A. A person who works hard their entire life should find some time to enjoy retirement while they still can.

Remember, big businesses got a windfall tax break under the previous administration. Well. I wouldn't take it all back. They got 14% off… I'd bring the rate down 7%. Then they can give 2% before taxes to support the ACA and 2% pretax collected by the Feds for the States for assistance with Medicaid programs and other programs for the underprivileged. The state funds collected for the year would be split in

March by population and sent to the governors with the manner of distribution to be approved by the state's congress. Personal returns would still be contributing the 2% on income over $600,000 to the ACA.

An IRS professional would review the tax laws to weed out any unreasonable items. I'm sure they'd find something.

If we adopt any sort of 'Medicare for All'- three tiers of monthly payments for those who *wish* to sign up and three tiers of co-pays, dependent on income and family size. The cost to seniors would remain the same. Your employer would deduct those payments as withholding or you could opt for direct payment. The law mandating medical insurance will be re-activated. You could assure the petty of the middle class that they won't have to worry about paying for the medical care of immigrants and slackers (smile).

Sketchy. A few more details to work out. It could work. We have to continue to reduce the cost of medical training and regulate student loans to help doctors and other healthcare personnel live amicably on the rates paid by Medicare. We will continue ramped up efforts to prosecute those who abuse the Medicare and market systems.

A lot of drugs we see as "American' made are in fact made by American companies owned in other countries. Or of foreign companies shipped to American packaging plants. The FDA must be a non-partisan, non-biased, above board uncompromised operation.

Why does the most important medicines cost so much less in other countries? To aid Medicare/Social Security/Medicaid and all those with other providers have quality care – and to persuade American companies to find a way to lower their prices, pharmacies should be allowed to stock these drugs with the government substantially lowering import costs. Ideally, the World Health Organization should be a go between, keeping up with all availability sources of certain drugs and providing that information to each country's CDC type organizations. It would drastically cut costs for Medicare, and lighten the burden for drug costs across the board.

In most states, Medi*caid* has 20 to 40 different programs. It's not efficient. Different areas do require different assistance, but programs should be narrowed down to 10-15 programs, with eligibility and benefits standardized.

We won't be able to solve the deficit and economic problems that fast. We can only hope we can fix some of it before the country hits bankruptcy and our dollar is devalued around the world. To show good faith, the federal government should decrease each agency's budget by 10%, to be reviewed in two years. The changes should be approved by the OMB, the President, and the Main Commitee. Congress should also decrease its' budget…by 15%, also to be reviewed in two years and approved by the OMB and the congressional Committee mentioned earlier. I'm sure a 3% salary decrease, a 10% decrease in expense and expense accounts, and a 2% cut in fixed cost of the congressional office building expenses could go almost unnoticed. (By the way, Congress should never again be allowed to set their own wages and expense accounts.) The Military and the justice and security departments can forgo celebratory functions or something similar that wouldn't be intrusive.

The states should also make a similar effort. They may have to anyway, looking at the underfunding of emergency items being experienced.

It goes without saying that any large industries who require funds to keep their business running would only get it under precise agreements for paying it back. I mean, who would even ask for anything else while our economy is in such decline?

Once we get all the corruption out of our government and remove the foreign interference we will heal and prosper, but it won't come overnight.

Some really believe the economy is great right now. Well, it isn't. The current administration has dumped trillions into Wall Street manipulating the status of the stock market to please their benefactors. I've actually heard people (black and white alike) say they don't care what this president does as long as their investments are doing well. How distasteful. They are in for a very rude awakening. They may lose not just their dividends and interest, but their principle as well when the crap hits the fan. The manipulation is not sustainable.

With a second term for the current administration, the US will be left in the condition most of the presidents' businesses were left in – bankrupt, unemployed, in great debt, with no credit. Of course Congress would be dismissed, Trump will be rich and Putin will have an office in the Whitehouse with staff living at Mar Largo with agents of Saudi Arabia.

I say this to point out that a new administration will experience the effects of the prior administration's policies for a couple of years before theirs manifests. Just as Trump had the great economy left by the Obama administration for a couple of years. We may see a worsening economy for a while – maybe a depression – and those things take a while to overcome. If we found money to dump into Wall Street, for the president and his minions to line their own pockets with taxpayer money, we can come up with money to make the citizenry whole again.

The government debt will rise even more at first– we can't wait for a great economy to aide all the people suffering from the effects of covid-19 and weather and fire catastrophes. It will get worse before it gets better. We need the 'better' to be sustainable.The covid-19 pandemic added an additional layer of strife to be dealt with in the next administration. The race to fortify infrastructure, generate green policies for energy conservation, and restructure education will be on hold for just a few months.

Pray. And remember that throughout history, when the economy tanked, a democrat inherited it and fixed it.

Hunker down and be patient. This too shall pass.

The Whining

Foreigners/Immigrants

It appears that foreigners have more respect for the American dream and the American system of democracy than Americans do. When they're able to make it here, they seem to work harder and instill more integrity into their work. They assist others coming in from their country with food and board and work, immediate family or not. They learn what legal and social assistance is available and *share* the information.

Immigrants seem to have more back bone than Americans. It makes sense because most of them have lived through harder circumstances and went through more to get here. Americans are *softer*. Almost spoiled. Definitely unappreciative and never satisfied.

And yet Americans are jealous of the success immigrants earn here.

Information about immigrant lives in America is often incorrect but readily believed. It's never mentioned how much income taxes they contribute to the country, with not all of the exemptions Americans get. Yes – immigrants that are not citizens pay taxes. Yes – most are not doctors or lawyers or wealthy, but the ones that are sweated to get there. It's not their fault you didn't do it. There were plenty of spaces open for you. And the immigrants that work low-level labor jobs have more appreciation for being able to work than an American ever would. We complain about them having an unfair number of some types of businesses. We believe they've taken over all the convenience stores, all the grocery stores, the gas stations, the liquor stores. Yes, they own many of these types of businesses, and a good amount of more lucrative businesses. With all the biases some Americans have toward them, they practically *had* to open their own businesses to be able to work. And to have work available for incoming relatives until they can find better employment or earn a degree. And why are all these businesses successful? Service. A different level of appreciation for customers, and real efforts towards integrity. Isn't that why you go there? Often when you see an immigrant at a gas station or other business – they may just be cheap labor, not owners.

Not all by no means, but a lot of American owned and run businesses (of both blacks and whites and long-term Americanized immigrants) act like they are doing you a favor letting you buy from them. And when American businesses give a family member a job, they often start them at the top, where incoming immigrants get the lowest level jobs and move up later. Different work ethics.

Immigrants love their children as much as you love yours. They make sacrifices to be able to send them to colleges. They want them to be safe and well fed. They seek to spare their children harassment. They don't have that snotty air of entitlement that a lot of Americans have.

We make fun of their languages and insist they don't speak it. Where's the compassion for a person escaping poverty and/or cruelties. Or just having a dream of something better. How long would it take *you* to learn a new language, no matter how much you wanted to or how much you are badgered? As if they are hurting somebody with it. Or are we just jealous because they can speak two languages to our one. We make fun of them, and are paranoid in thinking that while they talk in their language, they're making fun of *us*. We turn our noses up at their religions and customs. How narcissistic to insist everybody take your religion and discard theirs.

I wonder…if you moved to a foreign country for whatever reason – would you stop celebrating Christmas? Would you change from, say, Christianity to whatever religion was prominent there? Would you never wear the cloths you brought with you?

We want to commit to buying just American made. Well, there's a very small choice of items left of almost everything. You see the name of a trusted American company, but when you read the small print, it's made overseas and packaged here. Look closely at the labels on fruits and vegetables, on your cloths, on your cosmetics. Sure, there are things still made in America. Just not enough to fill the demands. You can buy local fruits and vegetables, but they don't grow enough to even feed their whole city. You can order things made in America, but not at the price you pay bulk dealers. Foreign countries have automobile factories. But when an American company buys the plant, it's an 'American' car just not made here.

So if you want to fix all this, you have to go through American business policies. Employers can get cheaper and more appreciative labor in other countries, with it being a living wage because the cost of living is cheaper. The countries are happy to have the jobs. There are less regulations, fewer 'palms to grease' and buts to kiss. Companies look at our government regulations, how they apply to some and not others, how competition influencers enter into it, and the high costs involved. They have to put up with the entitled workforce, with employee expense around 25% of total expenses. The decent unions and the narcissistic ones. It's a whole thing. We, as consumers, can't grasp the whole picture. We like good stuff that cost less. The commitment to buy only pure American fades fast.

Of course the younger immigrants over time take on more of our attributes, and by the third or fourth generation, no matter how they look, they *are* us.

Speaking of percentages, I have no doubt that a small percentage of them are not good citizens and with no intention of being. I tend to believe that percentage is a lot less than, say, the percentage of whites like that. Immigrants are happier to be here and anxious to do well.

Yet some whites and blacks alike, rich and poor, don't want them here.

Rich People

We snarl when we mention rich people. We think of that saying that 2% of the population have 98% of the wealth and we're mad.

But wait – besides wishing we were them – what's wrong with rich people? If a person worked hard and earned their fortune they deserve it. If a person did nothing and all of a sudden became rich, that money is rightfully theirs. If they came by it illegally, there will be consequences that don't concern us.

We often think rich people should be doing more for poorer people or more for the country. Why? You earn your money. Is it your *responsibility* to give parts of it to those less fortunate than you are? If you do something charitable you deserve praise. But if you spend your money on yourself - you don't deserve to be *punished*. So the same should go for other people's money. The jealousy is wasteful.

Rich people already pay more income taxes than the non-rich. A percentage of their income is a whole lot more money than that same percentage of our income. And if you look, you'll find that most rich people *do* in fact have philanthropic activities, often without recognition. They don't have to do it. Bill and Melinda Gates are worth around 90 billion and run a charitable foundation, as do many really prosperous people. Oprah Winfrey has done too much to mention – including operating an educational facility in a third world country for deprived girls. Sports celebrities have given back to poor neighborhoods, Ellen DeGeneres gives to various nonprofit organizations and rewards to needy individuals. Jeff and Mackenzie Bezos, Mike Bloomberg, Mark Zuckerberg, George Soros and other extremely rich people spend billions on philanthropic activity and have been doing so for years. Out of their pockets. The list goes on and on.

They can't be blamed for Trumps tax breaks. The ones listed above did not contribute (bribe) to that and don't support the administration. Of course they benefited, no reason not to.

You can't negate the good deeds of those less fortunate, either. A dollar in the bell ringers' pot, a ticket to a police or fireman's activity, giving blood to the Red Cross are all still philanthropic activities out of pocket that they didn't have to do. And they should be just as proud of their contributions.

Governments charge higher taxes and on the rich to assist the country because there's nowhere else to get it – not because they *should* be responsible for everybody else. And very few of them complain about it.

A lot of prosperous corporations award scholarships and support charities (although most of that came out of the high price we pay for their services and necessary community investments required by lenders or city/state officials). It still helps no matter why it's done, no matter how much is tax deductible. There are different levels of 'rich' and a lot more rich people than there used to be. Don't be a hater. (smile)

White People

I empathize with whites in America feeling overwhelmed by the protections and sympathies for blacks and foreign citizens. They feel like there are organizations for the benefit of different races and different religious sects, but nothing for them. While not identifying with it, they sometimes fall back on the KKK as the only group protecting whites. The problem is, the KKK aren't for benefitting whites, but for sending every other race into extinction. They want to make pure whites supreme. All the laws have always protected whites as they still do. It's just that humanitarian efforts have expanded the laws to protect others not *specifically* included before.

There seems to be fear of losing supremacy with the inclusion of so many non-whites and the fear of losing majority status. It should be noted that the other races aren't seeking supremacy. They don't wish to be better than anybody. They aren't asking for anyone to speak their language or take on their religion – they just seek inclusion and all the benefits and protections awarded everyone else. Doesn't that ease your mind? If you still have that latent need to be better than somebody, maybe the only way you know to raise your self-esteem would be to do all you can to make others appear worse. So you can *feel* supreme. It would be more helpful to you and society to address those issues that affect your self-esteem.

There are myths about the social costs that fall on you for blacks and immigrants. You'd be surprised at how many whites are supported by government programs. And you'd also be surprised at the low percentage of people that are *fraudulently* receiving benefits. This includes whites, black and 'others'. There are doctors, insurers, and other scam artists stealing from the system. And you forget to acknowledge all the benefits garnered by having the blacks and immigrants working in the economy and serving in the armed forces, not to mention the philanthropy involved.

I don't understand the cries from the middle class about The Affordable Care Act. After all the middle class whining about their tax dollars paying for the medical care of 'slackers', it should be noted that the ACA is funded by %2 of incomes over $600,000. You still whine as if you were paying for it and that 'those' people should work and pay for themselves instead of sitting around waiting for handouts. The ACA made people more responsible by charging a big monetary penalty if they didn't get insured. And then you applaud removal of that penalty? I'm sure there were a lot of whites paying that penalty or Trump would never have had it removed. It may interest you to know that a lot of blacks felt the same way, complaining that those who work hard had to pay for those who wouldn't.

Be a Christian every once in a while. Thank God for what *you have* and stop pissing on other people's blessings.

Stop whining.

You can't base an entire race on the bad behavior of a few of them. Each race is made up of many sects. Immigrants are from many different countries. They can't be lumped into one race called 'other'.

Live and let live. If you don't like a race of people, you shouldn't have to socialize with them or invite them to your home. That's your castle. No matter what race you are. We shouldn't try to force or guilt people into having 'friends' they don't want. If you're so timid and intimidated that you prefer to socialize with only your own kind, so be it. But you *do* have to treat others respectfully and equally in the workplace and in public spaces. You *must* obey the laws of the country involving liberties and protections. Period.

In reality, whites are quite a diverse group and of diverse heritages. America isn't known as the melting pot for nothing. There's whites of various ancestry - Polish, Irish, African (Caucasians), German, and European to name a few. I find the antipathy against immigrants ironic.

Black People

If I could talk to black people I'd say "You've come a long way!"

Blacks have excelled in almost every category. You can't turn on a television without seeing a black person, there are hundreds of movies and series with an all-black cast. A whole black network. Blacks with Emmys, Oscars, on walls and walks of fame. You have a great deal of the rich and well-to-do. Black models, black politicians, a black was president of the whole country – not some token black – but a qualified individual who did as great a job as any other president, if not better. Laws have elevated you. You own big and small businesses. You live all over the world. You've contributed to the country in *countless* ways.

Really, if whites or any other people don't want you in their club or restaurant or neighborhood – report them and screw it. There are countless others who welcome you. It will end up being *their* loss. If public places or businesses discriminate against you, there are laws to punish them and a lot of white sympathizers to impact their income. You don't need to beg for friends or to be liked.

Yes – there are still discriminatory practices and systemic racism and white nationalists. You rally against it, no longer alone. In time, more slights will be alleviated. You'll *never* stop working towards true equality.

Be honest. A lot of you are just as racist as some whites. You need to address your own bigotry –towards whites, immigrants, religions, etc. No halo on your heads.

Don't hold people liable for something their ancestors did. Sure a lot of individual whites are guilty of spreading hate, of discriminating against you, of trying to keep you down. But they are a minority now. The majority of white Americans don't support them anymore. So stop whining about 'white people' as a whole and 'white people' holding you back. Call out the specific players and businesses and cultists and systemic factors. You have recourse now.

There's no integrity in ignoring black on black crime.

Obviously, anal whites are not the only people preying on you. I always hear about being locked up for things white people have always done. That's a racist cop-out. If a black guy scammed you out of your life savings – would it be okay because white people did it? If a black serial killer murdered a bunch of people would you say, oh, just let him go, white people have been serial killers for years! Do you see how it sounds? Whatever race, if you do the crime, do the time. If you get caught, it's on you.

You often say 'buy black', do business with black companies. Support them. But when one scams you or does shoddy work, you don't want to say anything about it, falling back on the 'oh well, white people been doing it for years'. Then turning a nose up at blacks who decide to go elsewhere. That's a cop-out. Do you want to *be* like white people? Is it that unconsciously even you think white people are better than you? So after so many jack-leg black businesses mess over 'their own' a few times, a lot of blacks just turn the other way when they see an all- black business. The *quality* black businesses suffer because of it.

The prevalence of blacks in prisons has been brought to the country's attention and is being addressed. Keep your eye on that. But don't teach your children that they aren't responsible for their own actions because they are poor put upon descendants of slaves.

Remember and honor the plight of other people who have been tormented and/or enslaved because of their race. Just as bad as your ancestors had it. Jews encamped and murdered in gas chambers during the holocaust. Native American Indians encamped and having their land *and* children taken away. The Rwandan genocide. The 30,000 'disappeared' activists in Argentina. The human trafficking of disenfranchised people of any race for sexual exploitation, organ harvesting, house servants, slave labor, and other nefarious purposes still going on today and in many countries. The immigrants kept in cages, with their children snatched from them and also kept in cages. Living in filthy conditions and some just dying. Missing children, probably trafficked off somewhere.

Don't feel like the Lone Ranger. Thank God you made it this far.

There's hypocrisy in not joining others in protesting wrongful acts to people of other races. You should champion anybody that suffers mistreatment. For example, police officers who mistreat blacks are not all strictly racist, but sadistic towards any disenfranchised person of any race. They may unnecessarily beat a homeless person, or harass drug addicts or prostitutes, or small statured individuals. Taking up for all people's rights regardless of race will further legitimize your cause.

A lot of people labored to give you equality. A lot of them are white. Lincoln, who may have owned slaves as it was in those days, came to find slavery inhumane and stopped it. Some are offended by the black jockey statues on white people's lawns. But did you know they were a sign for safe stops along the underground railway? Many whites fought and died in the civil war that enforced Lincoln's decree to free slaves. For centuries there have been whites and others who stood up for you.

Sure, some whites weren't supportive, protecting their supremacy by blocking education and excluding higher level employment. But other whites prevailed. Black men became able to vote before women were, white or black. Many, many whites have helped your cause and are advocating for you even today. Right now.

Proud blacks worked diligently for our rights, many giving their very lives. I don't think they'd appreciate any blacks being an agent for segregation. They have broadened the places you can go and the peoples you can get to know. To enhance your life and expand your opportunities. Don't let black antagonists huddle you together under their wing and keep you from all that awaits you and heighten your hate of others that may not be your enemy. They want to make a name for themselves, they need followers, and before you know it – people lose interest and stop taking your premises seriously. The strides being made in the 'Black Lives Matter' initiative shouldn't be compromised by piggy-back grandstanders or rioters or inconsistent messaging.

You can't keep playing on white guilt. It's just getting old. You've received reparations – job quotas, college quotas, favorable business and housing loans, had token blacks installed in key places. You don't need forced inclusion anymore. Equal opportunity yes, but not pity participation. You can earn your accolades now. The pity card has been over-played and identifying with slaves is disrespectable to those who actually suffered through it. You don't have to vote for a person *just* because they are black – there are plenty of intelligent knowledgeable blacks available. You can vote for a white person or an immigrant or anybody they will represent your interests better. It's nothing more embarrassing to your race than to highlight the worst people you have to offer. You can stand on merit.

Even if you aren't all the way there – you've come a long way. Stop sometimes and be grateful for it and be appreciative of those who propelled you forward. All of them.

As with any race, there are multiple types of blacks. If you go into a business all loud, dropping trash, pants hanging off your butt and you feel people are being curt and annoyed towards you –they're not white racists - *ITS YOU*. Those blacks around you that some say are trying to be white or are snobbish because they're doing well and avoiding you– ITS YOU personally that they don't like. People are prejudice about many things. It's not the same as being racist. The same stands true for whites and immigrants.

Sometimes it's just not racism. Sometimes blacks aren't trying to be white – they just don't want to be stuck where you are. Your biases against them lowers the entire race. It's true.

Don't ever be a *mindless* sheep. Think for yourself and work as a team with like-minded individuals. The course of any life is not set in stone.

Focus

Consider all the things people of all races have in common. We all love our children. We all want education for ourselves and our children. We all have subsets in our race that are criminals or poor or rich, professionals and laborers, philanthropists and slackers and scammers. We all have family and friends who require help from government social programs. We all want to be safe. The more we all work together the better it will be.

You can say America is a Christian country. You can say America is a democratic society. You can speak of attaining the American Dream here. But practically, what trumps everything else, is that America is a *capitalist* Country. As are most countries.

I don't know what 'Christian' means anymore. Most who verbally call themselves Christians don't resemble anything of the definition I'd known. The word 'integrity' is an old forgotten word – not widely practiced in these times. Through the spread of international internet access, we find that the country we still love isn't all that they told us it was.

There will probably never be peace in the world. People who sell war weapons or want something that doesn't belong to them. Those manipulators of economies or the mentally & emotionally ill. The short-tempered or the sadists. They will not allow conflict or war to disappear.

There will always be racism. As time goes on, through cross breeding all skin colors will be basically the same. But human nature will find something else to object to, because most of the emotional or egotistical or capitalistic or envious straits we have today will transcend time. We will find something else to hate. It could be geographical or a 'class' system' or some other thing.

There will always be income disparities. Everybody cannot do the professional or most difficult jobs, somebody has to do the easiest or labor intensive jobs. But I do believe it's possible to blur the borders and provide everyone living wages, good healthcare, and good education.

Homelessness can be alleviated and *reputable* orphanages can be available to house children taken from abusive homes, indefinitely or with adoption possibilities - ways to save more of them and squash negative generational behavior cycles. Places where the children go to public schools and have lots of outside space and no stigmas attached to them.

Crime. That's a hard one. So many Americans feel demeaned or forgotten or have no recourse for being taken advantage of. Habitual criminals have risen exponentially due to modeling their criminal or abusive families or living through horrible situations. White collar crime goes mostly unpunished and perpetrators are treated like 'elite' criminals. America has the most murders of any other country. When you look at other countries where crime, including murder, are few and far between you find that the citizens aren't arms, all of the police aren't armed, and people have access to healthcare and education and employment. It will take a long time to have these things be acceptable to the narcissistic, egotistic, entitled, greedy, dispassionate Americans of today.

They will scream for things to happen but are too self-centered to do what they have to do to achieve those things.

American human nature.....

But we will *always* fight to work towards improving things and there will always *be* improvement.

Most of us will live through the covid19 pandemic, most of us will learn from it. This is *so* hard. But you will make it one way or the other. The worst part is not your kids missing school for a year. After all, some kids start kindergarten at age 5, some at age 6 and are not differentiated throughout their education. You wouldn't place your children in danger over it. Being stuck in the house, being alone or with your family all day-that's heavy. But you will endure that down to the last fingernail rather than risk yours and your family's health and lives. But losing your income – losing your savings, maybe your home, so stressed out you feel sick. *That's* what making you crazy and scared and reckless.

People who are making big paychecks that only work a few days a year and even then don't do much of anything in that job – are bickering over whether or not to help those who desperately need it. It's starting to be too late. Naturally they have never been in such a position, can't imagine how people let themselves be in such a position (you should always have enough saving to hold you for six months, your parents will bail you out, you can just borrow the money and pay it back later), and don't think you need more help - because many (actually less than 2% of the population) are conning the government, and because your job should open soon, the pandemic is under control and you should work and leave you children somewhere where they *may* be safe.

All irrelevant or false premises.

People have lost their homes and all of their possessions in tornadoes, house fires, floods, bombings, etc. and didn't have insurance. They couldn't get to their jobs, it was hard to get aid with no address, except a little help in shelters. Friends and family loss lives. Some people have lived in areas/countries rife with disease and no real doctor for miles and miles. Almost none of these people could go out to a store or talk on a phone or even drive away in their cars. They would have to leave their city/state to find relatives, most of whom have precarious income and space themselves, and some that didn't welcome them with open arms. I can't imagine what those people went through. And go through for months or years.

Six months of this. People dying. Conflicting information. Citizens that reject science and authority. Inciting racism even now. We know there will be an end. We just have no idea when. Hold on. You don't see it now, but you will make through this.

It's funny, we study history, but it appears we don't learn from it. We don't recognize similarities. A lot of people can't see how things that happened years ago reflect us today. You don't have to have a degree to have common sense. Listen to that voice.

People like to say Trump is a liar and a retard and a criminal and really stupid. When you think about it, he is too lazy to read, has the vocabulary of a ten year old, has the attention span of a rock, is an ultra-chronic habitual liar, and says the *stupidest* things. He is definitely an asset to Russia and Saudi Arabia.

 But he managed to con his way into the highest office in the land, line his personal pockets with billions of dollars at our expense, pimp the WH for his own businesses, operate brazenly above the law, coerce all the congressional republicans and a lot of republican governors and Mayors into submission, and got all of his crooked friends out of jail.

So who's stupid now?

Going forward, we will be bombarded with negative information on Joe Biden and his vice president – some true from eons ago, some almost true but professionally twisted, and a lot of made up lies. In the background, besides gerrymandering, closing voting locations, recruiting people to disrupt locations and tamper with results, ordering wrong-doing in the Post Offices and then pointing to it to invalidate the vote, providing statistical information to their Russian operatives – Trump and McConnell will be furiously trying to get some of their ominous tasks completed just in case they don't win. Boy, are the big money lobbyists and Putin going to be hopping mad if they don't.

The Republican Party *always* has to cheat in as many ways possible in order to win. Because they don't have anything anybody wants and no merits or accomplishments to boast. They, in fact, obstruct accomplishment. You may think that your vote doesn't count because of 2016. But 2 things: a wide enough lead voids the electoral vote. The Court has ruled that electoral votes must be given to the one who got the most votes in the state. Republican Governors may try to illegally assign these votes, so eyes are all over them, and it's a criminal offense. We may have to find a way to avoid using the post office to return our ballots.

Joe Biden is experienced and knowledgeable, honest, truthful, law-abiding. Those are extremely important things we need in the next president. He will get rid of the vast corruption in the Trump federal government and place people that are experienced and knowledgeable to run key agencies in the government. He will repair the economy and foreign relations. He will assist us with aid to get us through, in getting rid of this virus, and in returning our lives to some sense of normalcy. It won't happen overnight but our democracy and safeguards will be restored. A lot of damage has been done. So, no, not overnight.

And with that, I'll quit speaking.